Daylight fades, deep sleep
colors blinking, shouted words —
Awake before spring.

THN

For Antonio Alan

and our first Christmas in Finland

FILLIP WOKE UP ON CHRISTMAS EVE

Written by Tarja Helena Nevala
Illustrated by Tracey Taylor Arvidson

Text Copyright © 2022 Tarja Helena Nevala
Illustration Copyright © 2022 Post Street Press LLC
Published by Post Street Press LLC
6018 N. Post Street, Spokane, WA 99205

Library of Congress Control Number: 2022910511

Summary: A fly woke up in Nana's Christmas tree thinking her festive table
was a picnic made for him — causing Nana to make a clever choice.

ISBN paperback: 979-8-9853616-2-9
ISBN hardcover: 979-8-9853616-3-6

First printing 2022

Printed in the U.S.A.

www.tarjanevala.com
www.poststreetpress.com

# Fillip Woke Up
## On Christmas Eve

Written by Tarja Helena Nevala
Illustrated by Tracey Taylor Arvidson

When daylight fades in cooler days
and autumn colors glow,
some creatures, bugs, and crawling things —
must find a place to go.

They seek a safe and snuggly spot
where they can sleep or pause.
Through winter days and nights they snooze,
'til spring the landscape thaws.

Small Fillip also looked around
for his own snoozy space.
He slowly flew and buzzed about,
then found a cozy place.

He closed his eyes and curled up snug
as cold winds blew and blew.
He fell into a deeper sleep
while snowdrifts grew and grew.

His thoughts and dreams were sugar sweet,
of gooey goodies — yum! —
of parties, picnics, sunny days,
and slurping up a crumb.

One day his tree began to shake,
but Fillip did not flinch.
He did not hear the tromping sounds.
He did not move an inch.

Tramping, *tromping, closer,* STOMPING,

**mutter,** murmur, SMACK!

Chatter, *chatter*, CHOPPING, **SCATTER**,
HACKING, whacking, **CRACK!**

Soon Fillip's tree was pulled inside
and decorated too.
It was Nana's Christmas tree!
What did Fillip do?

The room was warm and brightly lit.
Fillip's bristles itched.
His feelers woke up with a start.
They wiggled, swayed, and twitched.

Fillip blinked with fly delight,
then yawned and stretched his wings.
He thought he was a lucky guy
to see such lovely things.

"Now spring is here!" he buzzed out loud.
"My eyes, what do they see?
Bright party stuff and tasty treats.
A picnic made for me!"

Then, grinning, Fillip spread his wings
and launched into the air.
His sleepy brain and wobble-flight
gave Nana one BIG scare!

"Mucho gusto!" Fillip said
and landed on a cake.
It was Nana's mantecada —
butter, sugar, bake!

"Oh, don't you know it's Christmastime!"
came Nana's sudden cry.
She waved her arms and shouted loud:
"GET OFF THE CAKE, YOU FLY!"

The mantecada was delish
and Fillip could not leave.
So there he sat a little while
and ate on Christmas Eve.

"Sweet treats like this," he hummed with joy,
"are made for flies like me.
Surely all will understand,
I'm welcome company."

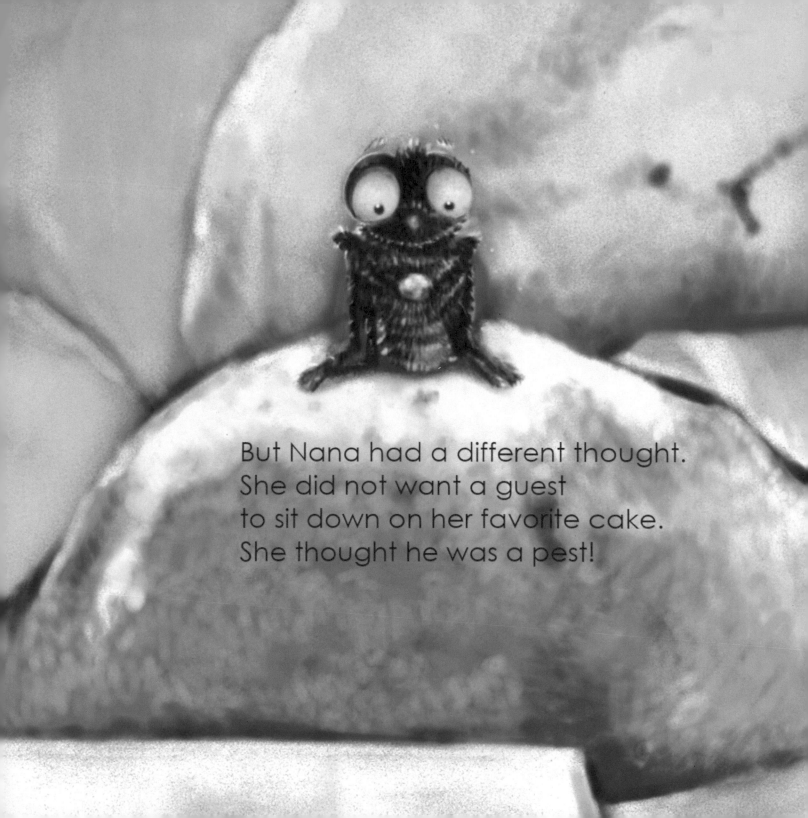

But Nana had a different thought.
She did not want a guest
to sit down on her favorite cake.
She thought he was a pest!

She scooped up Fillip with a spoon
and dashed across the floor,
then wondered what to do with him,
and bolted to the door.

"A Christmas feast you've had, old fly.
Now ádios, I say.
Go find another winter bed,
a cozy place to stay."

"Then stir again when spring arrives."
She waved her spoon up high.

"SHOO FLY!"

"SHOO NOW!"

"SHOO GO!"

She cried!

Small Fillip Buzzzzz

# Nana's Mantecadas

Mantecadas are like muffins. They taste somewhat like pound cake.

1/2 cup warm milk
1 teaspoon dry yeast
2 teaspoons sugar

1 cup all-purpose flour
1 tablespoon cornstarch
1 teaspoon baking powder
1/4 teaspoon salt

1/2 cup butter, softened
1 tablespoon olive oil
1/2 cup sugar
2 large eggs, room temperature
1 teaspoon vanilla extract

Sugar, for sprinkling

Muffin pan and liners (cupcake liners)

Directions:

Always ask an adult for permission and help before baking!

You will need three bowls.

In the first bowl, mix warm milk, yeast, and 2 teaspoons sugar. Stir. Set aside and let it rest in a warm place.

While the yeast is resting, line a 12-count muffin pan with paper liners.

Combine flour, cornstarch, baking powder, and salt into a second bowl. Stir and set aside.

In a large bowl, whip the softened butter, oil, and sugar until fluffy. Beat eggs one at a time into the butter mixture. Add vanilla extract and the milk/yeast from the first bowl. Stir.  Mix dry ingredients into dough.

Spoon dough into lined muffin pan and sprinkle sugar on top.

Turn oven to 400 degrees Fahrenheit.

Let the dough rest while oven is preheating, about 10-15 minutes.

Bake Mantecadas for 15 minutes.

Let cool and enjoy!

Mantecada is a popular Spanish cake that originated a few hundred years ago in Astorga, in northwestern Spain. They are a protected product as per Geographical Indication (Indicación Geográfica Protegida) by the European Union. Different versions of mantecada are enjoyed in many countries around the world.

# Fun fly facts

Fillip can taste with his feet and antenna-like feelers.

His feelers and bristles help him smell. He can smell food as far as four miles away. Fillip can smell quite well.

He has pads on his feet that help him walk upside down.

He cleans his feet by rubbing them together. Why do you think he does that?

Fillip has no teeth. He can't chew through a fly screen. He can't chew his food either. Fillip eats by slurping through his proboscis. A proboscis is like a drinking straw. When Fillip wanted to eat Nana's cake, he threw up on it first. Then, he waited for his spit and vomit to change the cake crumb into a liquid meal. Yuck!

There are many fly species in the world. We don't know which fly species Fillip belongs to. He acts like a musca domestica, but he slept in a fir tree during winter, and that is not musca domestica behavior. He is a funny fly.

Musca domestica flies, or house flies, are good for the environment but not good for you. Why?

Sometimes flies lay their small fly eggs into dirty, rotting, and often smelly waste. They even lay their eggs into poop! The eggs change into larvae, and the worm-like larvae eat the dirty waste. They help clean up the environment.

The fly larvae grow and then change into pupae. A new and fully grown fly develops inside one pupa. When the new fly is ready, it breaks out of the pupa shell and begins looking for something to eat. Flies can come from dirty places and may carry bad bacteria. If a fly lands on your food and you eat it, you could get sick from the bad bacteria. Yuck!

Some creatures, bugs, and crawling things, slow down or go to sleep when fall sets in. These changes are called diapause and hibernation. They are different from each other, but they both do the same thing. Diapause and hibernation help some creatures, bugs, and crawling things, to survive the winter.

We live in an amazing world!

CPSIA information can be obtained
at www.ICGtesting.com
Printed in the USA
BVHW022312031122
651101BV00001B/5